TO MY FAVORITE
CAT.
THING

Opi

How to Be a Cat

How to Be a Cat

Lisa Swerling & Ralph Lazar

CHRONICLE BOOKS
SAN FRANCISCO

Just be adorable.

Refuse cuddles at a reasonable time.
Demand them at 7 a.m.

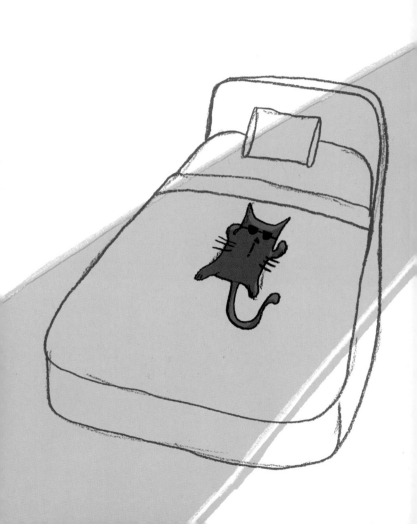

Soak up the rays in the sweet
morning light.

Consider it important to throw up
at 4 a.m. at least twice a month.
Preferably on the carpet.

Don't let your human go.
She MUST stay at home.

Never let your human pay more
attention to their book than to you.

Eat until you are sleepy and then sleep until you are hungry.

Jump on anything that moves
on the bed.

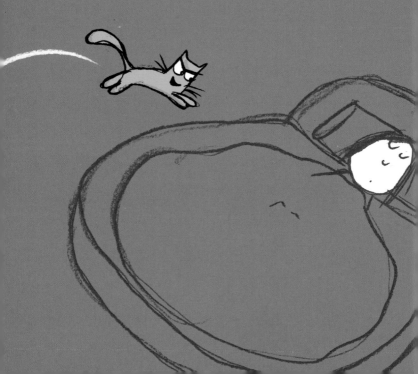

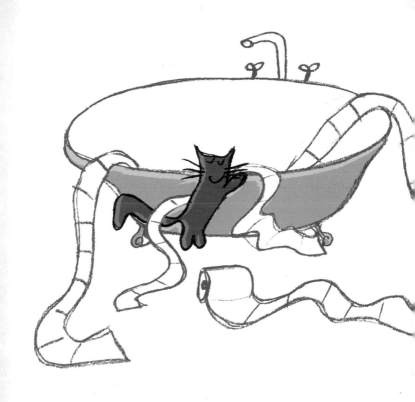

Don't be scared to decorate
the bathroom.

Dash for the door
as soon as it gets opened.

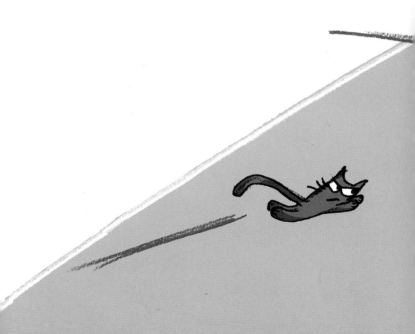

Never allow a human to close a door.
Especially not the bathroom door.
Ever.

Sleep anywhere.

A daily yoga session is
very important.

Jump ten feet in the air at the slightest sound in an otherwise quiet room.

Be a diva.

Stand and meow until your human
figures out what you want.
This can be hours of fun!

Be curious.

Beg for belly rubs, then attack your human after exactly three rubs.

A full stomach?
What is this curious concept?

Make yourself comfortable on your human's lap and remain there even after their legs go to sleep.

Sleep, sleep, and then sleep some more.
The more you sleep,
the catter you are.

Sit in front of the cabinet where your food is stored. Stare at it for extended periods.

When walking down the stairs in front of your human, stop suddenly to maximize their chance of tripping.

When your human is ill,
spend every second with them.

Walk over your human when they
are trying to sleep.*

* The face area of the human is
particularly rewarding to walk over.

Plants must be tasted.
Always.

Walk
elegantly.
Always.

When your photo is being taken, under
no circumstances stand still.

Assume every tin being opened
is full of tuna, just for you.

Look cute enough to
attract cuddles.

Sleep all day in a sunny spot.

Plead for food.
Once you have it, forget it.

From up high, watch your human
frantically look for you.
Say nothing.

When your human puts new sheets on the bed, add your own paw print design. Preferably muddy.

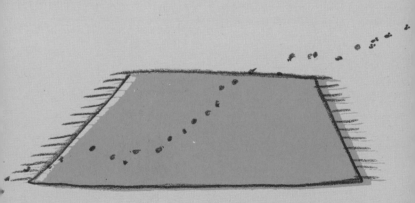

By all means play a bit of piano between 2 and 4 a.m.

Always be a cat, except when your human is in need of a best friend.

Insist your water bowl is freshly refilled EVERY time your human is nearby, even if that's every five minutes.

Be desperate to go outside, but when
the door is finally opened, refuse.

Start chasing a fly...

...then stop and sleep instead.

Always pounce on loose strings dangling from your human. They obviously put them there for a reason.

Be sure to let your human know they are sleeping on YOUR pillow.

Follow your human around the house,
by walking two steps in front of them.

Ignore the obvious scratching post.
Claw expensive furniture instead.

Randomly surprise attack your human
when they're gardening.

Refuse to be picked up when your
human tries to show guests how loving
and cuddly you are.

Knead the human till soft. If human tells you to stop, stop for three seconds. Proceed with kneading.

Always help the human save electricity.
A floor lamp should be on the FLOOR.

If your human wakes you up, show
that you are really annoyed...

...but it's never a problem to wake your human up. Really, they like it.

Seek out the visitor who hates cats.

Always sit on important looking documents. Your human will find this most helpful when looking for them.

1. Find box.

2. Stalk box.

3. Squeeze into box.

4. Destroy box.

5. Wait for next box.

Attack the carpet for no reason.

Then run away like crazy.

Share snuggles on cold nights.

It is important to enter
each shopping bag immediately
after your human empties it.

If your human wants to work, feel free to take a spontaneous laptop nap.

If you're a black cat, you must sleep on white clothing, and vice versa.

Pull at the roll of toilet paper. Hide in the pile. Play with the pile. Then look cute and expect to be praised.

The Christmas tree MUST
be attacked.

When called, go in the
opposite direction.

Start gazing suddenly at nothing.

Must get laser dot.
Must be destroyed.

Keep new visitors under
CONSTANT surveillance.

Bubbles MUST be attacked.

Sit and gaze at your food bowl as
though you have not been fed for days
(even if it is full).

Nudge your head into the cellphone when you're not getting enough attention.

As soon as someone gets up, grab their place and act as if you've been there for ages.

Consider life a never-ending belly rub.

Take center stage at mealtimes.

Seek out the warmest lap.

Perfect the telepathic wake up stare.

Observe.

When your human returns from a long
day at work, always be welcoming.

Ignore your cat food when more interesting human food is around.

Roll over as if you want your tummy
scratched, but then scratch the
human who attempts to do so.

Wait for clothes to be perfectly ironed, then it's very important to lie on them.

When your human is about to go to sleep, start telling him everything about your day.

Make your human love you more and
more with each passing day.

Rest whenever possible,
you deserve it.

Library of Congress Cataloging-in-Publication data is available.

ISBN 978-1-4521-3892-3

Manufactured in China

FSC
www.fsc.org
MIX
Paper from
responsible sources
FSC™ C104723

10 9 8 7 6 5 4 3 2 1

Chronicle Books LLC
680 Second Street
San Francisco, CA 94107
www.chroniclebooks.com